CONTENTS

A Celebration of the Seasons

These twelve seasonal celebrations share a common centerpiece. They surround the enjoyable custom of tea and the pleasures of tradition. Time and tea are meant to be shared with the friends you love—joining in celebration and uniting in community. In big groups and small intimate gatherings, when people come together, traditions and memories are created, nurtured, and enhanced.

I will share ideas along with each month's menu that will help you enrich your gatherings—tea customs, conversation starters, and party themes. But of course, the most important activity of all is just being together. Enjoy the ritual of gathering around a beautiful table, pouring tea for each other, sharing delicious food, and being kind to one another.

Tea was a tradition in my family when I was growing up. My mother and her sisters treasured their beautiful teapots and teacups and delighted in sharing teatime with others. Because my family is Jewish, we enjoyed our tea in the tradition of Eastern European Jews. But as I grew older, I was delighted to find that tea is a tradition that encompasses many cultures and many centuries.

My first experience of afternoon tea in the traditional British style came during a trip to

Canada, when Bob and I visited the beautiful Empress Hotel in Victoria, British Columbia—one of the most beautiful old hotels I have ever seen. I was enchanted by the lovely teatime we enjoyed there, and I sought to learn more about this delightful and soul-satisfying custom. The more I learned, the more interested I became. Now I enjoy my tea with fuller appreciation for the many centuries of tradition behind it.

Quite a few decades have passed since I first saw Mama pour a cup of tea with her sisters, since I received my first china cup as a wedding present, since Bob and I enjoyed that first afternoon tea at the Empress Hotel. So much time—yet some things grow better with age. I enjoy my tea now with a sense of history, a sense of kinship with those who have gone before me.

Holidays, celebrations, and traditions give us an opportunity to make each month joyful. Now is always the best time to start making every season bright with memories to soothe your spirit the rest of your days.

As the British say, "Let's take tea."

Emilie

January

A Twelfth Night Tea

A CELEBRATION OF NEW BEGINNINGS

*You are cordially invited to attend
A Twelfth Night Tea
and welcome in the new year
among friends.*

During the short days of January, fireplaces radiate good cheer from the corner of many living rooms across the country. Maybe you have just completed the ritual of replacing your old, worn calendar with an unblemished, clean one just waiting to be filled with notes, special days, and events to look forward to. If you are like me, this moment is one of amazement and a bit of melancholy. I am just not quite ready to let go of the holidays. Allow yourself time to revel in the afterglow of the season. Chances are your friends rushed through Christmas so quickly that they too are ready for an evening of celebration.

January 6, the twelfth day after Christmas, was in Elizabethan England the last day of the gala holiday season. This day can be set aside to culminate a long winter of festive events. What better way to serve up the spirit of beginnings than by gathering your friends together for a Twelfth Night tea?

Recipes

BASIC SCONES*

Scones are quite simple to make, so I usually make my own. However, a packaged scone mix can also give you very good results. You can add all kinds of extras to scones, depending on your taste. Try cut-up apples, currants, ginger, orange, almond flavoring, cinnamon, apricots, fresh blueberries, cranberries, or even chocolate chips.

2 cups flour
1 tablespoon baking powder
2 tablespoons sugar
1/2 teaspoon salt
6 tablespoons butter
1/2 cup buttermilk
lightly beaten egg

Mix dry ingredients. Cut in 6 tablespoons butter until mixture resembles coarse cornmeal. Make a well in the center and pour in buttermilk. If you don't have buttermilk, use regular milk. Mix until dough clings together and is a bit sticky—do not overmix. Turn out dough onto a floured surface and shape into a 6- to 8-inch round about 1 1/2 inches thick. Quickly cut into pie wedges or use a large round biscuit cutter to cut circles. The secret of tender scones is a minimum of handling. Place on ungreased cookie sheet, being sure the sides of the scones don't touch each other. Brush with egg for a shiny, beautiful brown scone. Bake at 425° for 10 to 20 minutes, or until light brown.

To transform this basic scones recipe into one for herb scones, just add about 3 tablespoons of fresh (or 1 tablespoon dried) herbs (basil, thyme, oregano). Serve with softened butter mixed with chopped herbs and a dash of lemon juice.

SPICED PEARS

7 large pears
1 cup apple juice
1/2 cup sugar
1/2 cup fruit vinegar
2 teaspoons cloves
1 cinnamon stick
1 teaspoon peppercorns
2 bay leaves

Peel, core, and halve the pears. Combine apple juice with sugar, fruit vinegar, and whole spices. Simmer until the sugar is dissolved; add pears, turn off heat, and let them cool in the liquid. Drain well before serving. Serves 14.

Create in me a pure heart,
O God, and renew a
steadfast spirit within me.

PSALM 51:10

TANTALIZING TRIFLE

Trifle is a wonderful English dish, perfect for tea!

5 peaches, peeled and sliced
$^2/_3$ cup plus 2 tablespoons peach schnapps
1 5" x 9" pound cake, purchased or
   homemade
fresh berries for garnish
10 ladyfingers
 Peach Cream
1 cup whipping cream
2 tablespoons sugar

Brush flat sides of ladyfingers with $^1/_3$ cup of peach schnapps and line the sides and bottom of a glass serving bowl with 8 to 10 cup capacity. Spoon half of the Peach Cream over the ladyfingers lining the bottom of the dish. Arrange half of the peaches on top of the Peach Cream. Slice cake lengthwise into $^1/_2$-inch slices and brush cake slices on both sides with $^1/_3$ cup schnapps. Arrange half of the cake slices on top of peaches. Repeat layers of Peach Cream, peaches, and cake slices. Whip cream until medium soft peaks form. Add sugar and 2 tablespoons schnapps and continue beating until blended. Spread cream mixture over the top of trifle and garnish with fresh berries. Wrap tightly with plastic wrap and refrigerate overnight. Makes 8 servings.

PEACH CREAM

8 egg yolks
$2^1/_4$ cups half-and-half
3 tablespoons peach schnapps
6 tablespoons sugar
4 teaspoons cornstarch

In medium bowl, beat egg yolks until thickened. Gradually add sugar and beat until mixture is thick and lemon-colored. Pour into a saucepan and beat in 2 cups half-and-half. Mix cornstarch with remaining half-and-half and beat into egg mixture. Cook over medium-low heat and stir constantly until mixture thickens (6 to 8 minutes). Do not let mixture boil. Remove from heat and stir in the peach schnapps. Cool to room temperature and then chill. Mixture will thicken more as it cools.

You're Invited...

First impressions matter! The way you invite friends to a tea party will encourage them with that first spark of anticipation. Victorian invitations to tea were works of art in themselves, extravagantly engraved on white paper. Your delicate touch can be as simple as hand lettering (with calligraphy, if you know it) your personal invitation on stationery that reflects the theme you have planned. Add glitter, confetti, or other festive touches. Keep the wording simple so that your welcoming spirit shines through clearly.

Twelfth Night Tradition Activity

William Shakespeare chose "Twelfth Night" as the name of one of his most boisterous comedies. Tell your guests they're invited to a play reading, and then collect as many copies of Shakespeare's play from the library as you can. Put the name of the 14 characters on slips of paper and ask each guest to draw one. (If you have fewer than 14 guests, one person can take two minor roles.) For those rusty on their Shakespeare, give a short summary of the plot, and then let the play begin.

MAGGIE STUCKEY

A Touch of Inspiration

A Twelfth Night tea allows for much creativity. Play up the Elizabethan theme by wearing period costumes and decorating with English flair. Or keep your decor simple and fresh with aromatic arrangements of colorful fruit alongside clusters of cinnamon, cloves, and other spices. Spread an embroidered tea cloth on a table or a tray and use the nicest pot and cups you have. Introduce texture and opulence to your table by intertwining velvet or brocade scarves with your centerpiece. Light a candle and set a little gift (a card, a small decorative object, a copy of Shakespeare's *Twelfth Night*) at each friend's place setting.

Set your mood and the ambience for the gathering by playing classical music as you prepare the room and as guests arrive. When friends enter your home, have them pause to write down on a slip of paper one resolution they have for the new year. Later in the evening, read these out loud and let the group guess who submitted the resolution. Or in the spirit of the play *Twelfth Night*, a romantic comedy replete with mistaken identities, ask each person to make their own calling card for the year by finishing this statement on their slip of paper, "In the new year, I want to be more like…"

Keep the fireplace burning and the scented candles lit. The illumination of these flames will be a gentle reminder of the hope wrapped in new beginnings and the brightness of a season spent with dear friends.

February

A Valentine's Day Tea

A CELEBRATION OF LOVE

Let us gather for a Valentine's Day tea.
Bring someone you love to join us for
delicacies, tea, and fond memories.

When did February 14 become a celebration of the heart for you?

I vividly recall one year in elementary school when Cupid's arrow pricked my heart. With great anticipation I selected and signed a special card and enjoyed the thrill of communicating my heart for the first time.

Many decades later I still look at Valentine's Day as a chance to express love and affection to those dear to me. What a wonderful occasion to shower friends and your special someone with cards, candy, flowers, poetry, and my favorite gesture of kindness—a Valentine's Day tea.

This celebration is a day of love, so have your guest bring with them a person they love. It might be a husband, a parent, a child, a neighbor, a friend, a significant other. Ask each invited guest to bring a photo featuring themselves with their friend. The picture might be of a wedding or a honeymoon, a parent with their child, a child growing up, or friends working side by side or smiling on a shared vacation. Blend these images into your table decor. At a later time during the tea, have each guest tell about their friend and the story behind the picture. Sharing these reflections becomes a way of passing along love's sublime gifts throughout our many seasons.

Recipes

SWEETHEART SANDWICHES

sliced turkey
¼ cup Dijon mustard
1 can whole cranberry sauce
1 loaf sourdough bread

Mix the mustard and cranberry sauce together to create a delicious blend. Smooth onto bread of choice and add sliced turkey. Cut sandwiches with a heart-shaped cookie cutter.

PASSION FRUIT TARTS

ready-made pie crust
strawberries
kiwis
bananas
½ cup cold passion fruit juice
    (or apple juice)
1 tablespoon cornstarch

First, make tart shells. Roll out your favorite piecrust about ¼ inch thick (or thinner). Cut circles 1 inch wider than your muffin tins and fit them into the bottoms of the tins and partway up the sides. Prick bottoms with a fork. Bake at 350° until lightly brown (about 10 minutes). When cool, fill each to the top with fresh fruit: strawberries, kiwis, bananas. To make a glaze, in a small saucepan mix the cold passion fruit juice with cornstarch and simmer over medium heat until juice is clear and thickened. Spoon over fruit and refrigerate until glaze sets (at least one hour). Makes ½ cup glaze; enough for six 3-inch tarts.

Legends of Love

No one is quite sure who St. Valentine was. The early lists of church martyrs reveal at least three people named Valentine, each of whom had his feast day on February 14. Various legends have come down to us, too. Valentine was said to have been imprisoned, and while there, he cured the jailer's daughter of blindness. Another story, in an attempt to associate Valentine more closely with Valentine's Day, has him falling in love with the jailer's daughter and sending her a letter which he signed, "From your Valentine."

time, beating well after each addition. At low speed, beat in cocoa and almond extract until blended. Fold in almonds, reserving 1 tablespoon. Drop mixture by slightly rounded tablespoonfuls onto cookie sheets. Sprinkle tops with reserved almonds. Bake 1 hour and 15 minutes or until set. Cool the cookie sheets on wire racks for 10 minutes. With a metal spatula, carefully loosen and remove kisses from foil; cool completely on wire racks. Store in tightly covered container. Makes about 2 dozen kisses.

HEART-SMART COCOA KISSES
Light as air, low-fat cookies for you and your Valentine.

2 egg whites
1/4 teaspoon cream of tartar
1/8 teaspoon salt
2/3 cup sugar
3 tablespoons cocoa
3/4 teaspoon almond extract
1/3 cup finely chopped almonds

Preheat oven to 200°. Line 2 large cookie sheets with foil. In small bowl with mixer at high speed, beat egg whites, cream of tartar, and salt until soft peaks form. At high speed, gradually beat in sugar, 2 tablespoons at a

FRESH STRAWBERRY BLOSSOM TEA

40 fresh strawberries (tops only) rinsed
2 cups of cold water

Preheat oven to 150°. Remove the green leaves from the tops of the strawberries. (Reserve berries for other strawberry recipes.) Spread the leaves out evenly on a baking pan. Place in oven for 10-15 minutes or until leaves are dry and crumbly. Bring 2 cups of cold water to a boil. Remove from heat and immediately add dried leaves. Cover and set aside in a warm place for 7-10 minutes. Strain and serve. Makes 2 cups.

A Touch of Inspiration

Dress this tea party in the colors of love: red, pink, and white. Cover your table with oh-so-soft red and white flannel or use a cotton sheet in a tender shade of pink. Sprinkle candy hearts around the table settings and scatter them generously around the house. Burn candles in scents of vanilla and peppermint for a soothing and romantic ambience.

Cut out heart shapes in colored paper and write a few lines of encouragement for each guest. Tell them why they are loved. Write a verse of Scripture, a poem, or an original sentiment. Place them around the room so your guests can find them as they mingle with each other.

The teatime conversation should embrace the love theme. Invite the married women to share how they met and married their husbands. Get personal and tell of God's love in your life. Let this truly be a time to share from the heart. And most of all, let it encourage others to pass along the legacy of love as part of their own family tradition.

Valentine's Day Tradition

The English settlers in the New World brought their Valentine customs with them. Prior to the eighteenth century, some colonists exchanged simple homemade Valentine cards. But after 1723, the custom really began to grow with the influence of English Valentine writers. Commercial Valentines appeared by about 1800, and by 1840 they were becoming sophisticated. Brew your favorite flavor of tea and enjoy an afternoon of making or writing on Valentine's Day cards to tell your friends and family that you love them.

March

The Feast of Easter

A CELEBRATION OF JOY

We request the pleasure of your company
for an Easter brunch.
Let us gather and rejoice.

The feast of Easter was well established by the second century. In A.D. 325, the Council of Nicaea decided that Easter should fall on the Sunday following the first full moon after the vernal equinox.

In the early church, the several days called Pascha commemorated the passion, death, and resurrection of Jesus Christ. By the fourth century, Pascha Sunday had become a separate day that commemorated the resurrection.

The contemporary tradition of Easter includes fluffy bunnies, pastel-colored versions of your favorite name-brand candy, egg hunts in parks and neighborhoods, and new Sunday outfits adorned with sashes and ribbons. I believe these cheerful pleasures resonate with the message of joy born in the Easter tradition. I encourage you to celebrate the wonders of spring that usher in this Easter joy. This season becomes an opportunity to embrace treasures of faith, friendship, and feasting. May the essence of the Pascha inspire you to gather together with those you cherish.

Let the feasting begin! Hallelujah.

Recipes

TURKEY SAUSAGE

Mix together thoroughly with a fork:

1 pound ground turkey
1 teaspoon salt
$^1/_2$ teaspoon nutmeg
$^1/_2$ teaspoon sage
$^1/_2$ teaspoon thyme
$^1/_8$ teaspoon cayenne pepper

Shape into 12 small patties. Fry in ungreased skillet or bake at 350° for 10 to 15 minutes in shallow pan until done. Do not overcook or patties will become tough. Oven baking produces juicier patties and is easier when feeding a crowd. Makes 12 patties (serves 6).

OVEN-BAKED SPINACH MUSHROOM FRITTATA

1 bunch spinach, washed
2 tablespoons melted butter
1 cup sliced fresh mushrooms
2 green onions, chopped
6 large eggs, beaten
6 tablespoons water or milk
$^1/_4$ teaspoon salt
8 ounces cream cheese, crumbled into small pieces

Steam, drain, and chop spinach; sauté onions and mushrooms in butter until barely tender. Combine remaining ingredients in order given. Stir in the vegetables and pour into well-buttered 9" x 13" pan. Bake at 350° for 35 minutes or until a knife comes out clean. Serve as desired with avocado wedges or salsa. Makes 6 to 8 servings.

Easter Tradition

One of the beautiful religious customs of Easter is the sunrise service held by many Christian denominations. These services may well have their origin in the biblical text: "But on the first day of the week, at early dawn, they came to the tomb" (Luke 24:1 NASB). The outdoor Easter service was brought to America by Protestant emigrants from Moravia. The first such service in America was held in Bethlehem, Pennsylvania, in 1741.

Find out which churches have a sunrise service in your area. Go with your spouse, family, or a friend to enjoy the music and the message of Easter joy.

STRAWBERRY COCONUT SURPRISE MUFFINS

A delightful breakfast, dessert, or snack muffin.
Best served warm.

1 cup buttermilk
1 cup uncooked rolled oats
1 egg
1/4 cup honey or crystalline fructose
    (health-food store)
3/4 cup shredded coconut, unsweetened
    (health-food store)
1 cup whole wheat pastry flour
    (health-food store)
1 1/2 teaspoons baking powder
    (low-sodium baking powder from
    health-food store preferred)
1/2 teaspoon baking soda
1/2 teaspoon salt
1/4 cup strawberry preserves

Spray muffin pan with no-stick cooking spray (Olive Oil Pam Spray preferred). Blend together buttermilk and rolled oats and let stand for 30 minutes. Then blend in coconut, honey, and egg. In a separate bowl, blend together remaining dry ingredients.

Combine dry ingredients with liquid ingredients just until mixed. Do not overmix. Fill muffin cups about half full. Place in center of each: 1 scant teaspoon strawberry preserves. Cover preserves of each muffin with dab of remaining dough. Bake at 400° for 20 minutes. Cool 2 minutes or longer (until muffins come out of pan easily). Makes 10 medium muffins.

HERBAL TEA

With the rich flavors on the menu, serve complementary mild hot drinks of regular and decaffeinated coffee and spiced herb teas. Purchase three or four choices of teas that are individually packaged in colorful wrappers. Put a pot of piping-hot water on the table with a tray or bowl of herbal tea bags, allowing guests to choose and prepare their own. Provide honey, cream, and lemon wedges.

There is only one way to bring peace to the heart, joy to the mind, and beauty to the life; it is to accept and do the will of God.

WILLIAM BARCLAY

Brewing a Perfect Pot of Tea

Preparing a perfect cup of tea takes time! But these little steps can make the difference between a mediocre cup of tea and an excellent one.

- Empty the teakettle and refill it with freshly drawn cold water. Put the kettle on to boil.
- While the kettle is heating, pour hot water into the teapot to warm it. Ceramic (china, porcelain, stoneware) or glass teapots work best; tea brewed in a metal teapot may have a metallic taste.
- Pour the hot water out of the teapot and add the tea. Measure a spoonful of loose tea for each cup desired into the warmed (empty) teapot, plus one extra spoonful for the pot. (Most teapots hold five to six cups.) If you are using tea bags, use one bag less than the desired number of cups. Put the lid back on the pot.
- As soon as the kettle comes to a rolling boil, remove from heat. Overboiling causes the water to lose oxygen, and the resulting brew will taste flat.
- Pour boiling water into the teapot, cover, and let the tea brew from three to six minutes. Small tea leaves will take less time to brew than large ones.
- Gently stir the tea before pouring it through a tea strainer into the teacups. If you used tea bags, remove them.

19

A Touch of Inspiration

Let the celebration of joy begin with a feast for the eyes. As guests cross your threshold, offer their senses a banquet of delights. Chase away any remnants of winter's cold with a display of jubilant hues: elegant taper candles, spring bouquets, and rooms graced with traditional symbols—Easter lilies, baskets of tulips, and crosses adorned with a single wreath of flowers.

For your table setting, start with a pink tablecloth with a white or ecru lace cover, allowing the pink to show through. If a lace cover is unavailable, white or ecru place mats can be used with contrasting pastel-colored napkins. Adorn each napkin with a flowered napkin ring or a single spring flower. At each place setting put a silver or white porcelain eggcup filled with a pastel-colored candle to be lit at the beginning of the meal.

Reflect light as your centerpiece. Set an oblong mirror in the center of the table and place a silver candelabra or silver candlesticks with tall pink candles on the mirror's glass surface. Float flower blooms in crystal bowls filled with water. Even ornate drinking glasses provide a sweet resting place for a single blossom.

Begin your preparations with a mind and heart set on the Easter tradition of joy. You will feel a sense of peace as you take care of the loving touches. And when your guests arrive, they too will feel the tranquility of your heart.

May the God of hope fill you with all joy

and peace as you trust in him.

ROMANS 15:13

20

April

A Spring Fling Tea

A CELEBRATION OF FRIENDSHIP

*By official invitation your
presence is requested
to attend a gala celebrating
the beginning of spring.*

I find waiting for spring difficult. In Southern California we are not buried under piles of snow or sawing holes in ice-covered lakes, but we do long for the fresh new season, when our days get longer, warmer, and new growth breaks through the ground.

I look forward to picking the first daffodils, hearing the new songs of the birds, and watching the earth sparkle after a spring rain. I sit back and watch while nature orchestrates a new beginning that evokes feelings of wonder. This cycle is so universal and yet so personal, it is my reminder to celebrate life.

This tea party honors spring as a special occasion. Fill this day with new memories and perhaps new friends as well. What an opportunity to invite a few people who you would like to get to know better. Spring is a great time to plant new friendships and watch them blossom in the seasons ahead.

I'd like to be the sort of friend that you have been to me;
I'd like to be the help that you've been always glad to be;
I'd like to mean as much to you each minute of the day
As you have meant, old friend of mine,
To me along the way.

EDGAR A. GUEST

Recipes

TOMATO BASIL SANDWICHES

$1/2$ cup unsalted butter, cut up

1 teaspoon tomato purée

$1/4$ teaspoon sugar

$1/4$ teaspoon salt

$1/8$ teaspoon pepper

$1/4$ teaspoon lemon juice

$1/4$ cup lightly packed chopped fresh basil
   or
1 tablespoon dried fresh basil

1 pound fresh tomatoes

8 slices white bread, crusts removed

8 slices whole wheat bread,
   crusts removed

salt and freshly ground pepper to taste

To make the basil butter, combine butter, tomato purée, sugar, salt, pepper, and lemon juice in a food processor. Process until blended. Add basil leaves. Pulse with on/off turns until blended. Set aside at room temperature. To make the filling, with a small knife, cut a small cross in bottom skin of each tomato. Place tomatoes into boiling water 20 seconds. Cool in cold water. Drain. Peel, core, and seed tomatoes. Chop tomato flesh very fine. Stir gently in strainer to drain. Just before serving, spread one side of each slice of bread with basil butter. Spread tomato filling on each slice. Season with salt and pepper to taste. Cut each sandwich in half. Serve fresh. Serves 16.

Ready or Not

The more prepared you are for hosting a tea, the more opportunities you will have to share the gift of hospitality with a friend or neighbor. Here are some basic items to start gathering in a special cupboard or even a basket.

Teakettle
Teapot
Tea strainer
Two teacups with saucers
Sugar bowl (or honey server)
Cream pitcher
Two small dessert plates and
    serving plates
Two teaspoons
Pretty tea cloth or large placemat
Two serviettes (cloth napkins)
Loose tea or good quality tea bags
Sugar cubes or honey
Lemon

LEMON BARS

2 cups flour
½ cup powdered sugar
1 cup butter
4 eggs
6 tablespoons lemon juice
2 cups sugar
6 tablespoons flour
1 teaspoon baking powder

Mix 2 cups flour, powdered sugar, and butter as pie crust. Pat smooth in 9" x 13" pan. Bake 20 minutes at 350° (less for glass pan). Mix eggs, lemon juice, sugar, flour, and baking powder together and pour over crust as it finishes baking. Bake 20 minutes more. Sprinkle powdered sugar while hot. Cut into squares.
Serves 12.

LEMON MINT TEA

2 quarts water
2 tablespoons lemon tea
2 teaspoons mint tea
6 to 8 lemon slices

In a large saucepan, bring the water to a full boil. Add the tea either loose or in a fine mesh infuser. Cover and let the tea stand for 5 minutes. Strain and transfer tea to the serving teapot. Have lemon slices available for those who would like.
Serves 6.

A Touch of Inspiration

As the green world awakens all around you this month, bring a bit of that dazzle into your home for the Spring Fling party and beyond. The colors that fill your yard can transform your party setting into a kaleidoscope of yellow, gold, and green hues. Think of daisies as you decorate, and you are sure to inspire smiles. Use a green tablecloth as your foundation and plant a garden of spring colors. Arrange pastel or primary-colored bright plates mismatched and bold, vases filled with green tinted water and clusters of daisies or silk white tulips, and sunshine yellow streams of ribbon curled about the base of each glass and place setting.

Now your home is ready to receive a group of special friends or friends-in-the-making. Maybe you decided to invite all new friends. Spring will breathe its fresh new life into all of your relationships.

The awe you experience when spring's flowers make their first appearance is the same sense of great possibility you discover in every new friendship. Where will this unique relationship take you? How will it feed your spirit and make you grow? How will you nurture it to make it stronger? And what color will it add to your life's garden?

Aren't such discoveries wonderful to look forward to?

The Art of Conversation

To blend new friends and old, inspire engaging conversation with these starter questions.

- Where did your family live when you were six? When you were twelve?
- What is the most valuable thing you've learned in the past ten years?
- What is the most encouraging word anyone can say to you?
- What is the greatest gift you have ever received?
- What's your idea of a truly perfect morning? What would you do?

May

A Mother's Day Tea

A CELEBRATION OF WOMEN

*You are invited to a gathering
of wonderful women.
Bring your daughter or mother for this
jubilant tea in honor of motherhood.*

Mother's Day is a time for handmade cards from little ones and flowers or long distance phone calls from older children. It is a time when a woman's heart beats with great pride and love for those she calls her children. Celebrate these women—yourself included—with a time of tea, conversation, and reflection.

As you invite mothers to this tea, encourage them to bring pictures of themselves as young girls. Display them on the table as centerpieces. The others can go around the tables and try to match the guest with the picture. Make moms feel special today.

Mother's Day is an occasion warm and joyful in spirit. Greetings are designed to be sent not only to one's own mother but also to grandmothers, aunts, mothers of wives and sweethearts, and to anyone who merits the accolades of motherhood. Expand your tea to include women who are away from their own mothers or children. Create a day to remember.

The Mother's Day Tradition

The first Mother's Day observance was a church service held in Grafton, West Virginia, on May 10, 1908, to honor motherhood and pay homage to Mrs. Anna Reese Jarvis. Her daughter, Anna M. Jarvis, was instrumental in establishing this day to honor mothers in general and also to honor her own mother.

By 1911 every state in the Union had adopted its own day for the observance of Mother's Day. On May 9, 1914, a resolution providing that the second Sunday in May be designated Mother's Day was issued by President Woodrow Wilson.

Take time to honor your own mother or perhaps an adopted mother with a special card, poem, prayer, or a special time to enjoy each other's company.

Honor...your mother so that you may live long.

EXODUS 20:12

Recipes

CHICKEN ALMOND SANDWICHES

1 cup chopped cooked chicken
½ cup slivered almonds, toasted
½ cup heavy cream
salt and freshly ground pepper to taste
8 slices white bread, crusts removed
8 slices whole wheat bread,
   crusts removed
chopped toasted almonds for garnish

In a blender, combine chicken, almonds, heavy cream, salt, and pepper. Blend at low speed until spreadable. Spread one side of each slice of bread with mustard butter (see following recipe). Spread chicken filling on buttered bread. Cut sandwich in half. Spread butter along one edge of sandwich. Press chopped almonds along edge to garnish.

MUSTARD BUTTER

½ cup unsalted butter, cut up
1 tablespoon mild French mustard
1 teaspoon lemon juice

In a food processor, combine butter, mustard, and lemon juice. Process until blended. Set aside at room temperature.

EMILIE'S CHOCOLATE BUNDT CAKE

½ cup sugar
¾ cup water
¾ cup oil
4 eggs
1 small carton sour cream
1 package chocolate pudding, instant
1 box yellow cake mix
1 package chocolate chips
powdered sugar

In a bowl, mix sugar, water, and oil. Mix in remaining ingredients. Pour into sprayed Bundt pan. Bake 350° for 1 hour. Cool 1 hour and put on cake plate. Top with powdered sugar and whipped cream.

Thank You, God...

...for pretending not to notice that one of Your angels is missing and for guiding her to me. You must have known how much I would need her, so You turned Your head for a minute and allowed her to slip away to me. Sometimes I wonder what special name You had for her. I call her "Mother."

BRAD, MY SON, IN A MOTHER'S DAY CARD

A Loving Recipe for a Perfect Cup of Tea

One willing friend who loves to sit and share

One grateful heart to have a friend that cares

One beautiful garden to show us God is near

Many wonderful memories of times shared throughout the years

Lots of smiles and laughter to brighten up our days

Many prayers that we prayed for each other along the way.

AUTHOR UNKNOWN

WHIPPED CREAM

1 cup whipping cream
1 tablespoon vanilla
2 tablespoons powdered sugar

Place a medium or large mixing bowl with beaters in the freezer for at least 2 hours (better yet, overnight). Take bowl and beaters from freezer, pour in 1 cup of whipping cream. One cup of cream makes 2 cups when whipped. Whip with electric mixer on high until the cream makes peaks (stiff). Just before the peaks come, add 1 tablespoon of vanilla. Add approximately 2 tablespoons of powdered sugar to taste. Serve with chocolate cake.

TANGERINE TEA

4 tangerine slices*
12 whole cloves
4 sticks of cinnamon
2 tablespoons sugar
4 cups orange pekoe tea brewed with the rind of one tangerine

Stud each slice of tangerine with 3 cloves. Now place a tangerine slice, a cinnamon stick, and 1½ teaspoons sugar in each cup. Fill with hot tea from the pot. Serve, using the cinnamon stick to stir the tea. Makes 4 cups.
*orange slices could also be used

As a mother comforts her child, so will I comfort you.

ISAIAH 66:13

A Touch of Inspiration

Enjoy the fun and satisfaction that comes from creating a beautiful setting just for the friends of your heart. Flowers, flowers, flowers. Fill every vase you have with flowers and then find alternative vases like carafes, pitchers, and attractive bottles and fill them with flowers. Roses, carnations, tulips, lilacs, lilies…anything that is in season in your area. Let the brilliant shades of color and exotic fragrances blend together. Mix and match so that each bouquet of flowers represents the many beautiful women who are known as "mother" to someone special.

A wonderful, easy gift to make is a floral bookmark for each woman. Place small, pressed flowers on a strip of colored paper and then add a favorite verse, poem, or reflection using your best penmanship or calligraphy. Laminate these at a local copy shop. Punch a hole at the top of each and then slip through a delicate strand of lace, satin, or silk ribbon. Tie it with a loop and display across each woman's plate surrounded by sprigs of fresh flowers.

To keep the conversation going, have each woman express what "mother" means to them by completing the acrostic M-O-T-H-E-R. The group will find many unique and wonderful definitions and interpretations to reflect on. As personal stories about mothers and motherhood fill the afternoon, this extraordinary day becomes a time of encouragement, support, and honor. Keep the tea flowing and the tissues handy.

Women like to make sacrifices in one big piece, to give God something grand.
But we can't.
Our lives are a mosaic of little things, like putting a rose in a vase on the table.
Sometimes we don't see how much those things mean.

INGRID TROBISCH

June

A Bridal Tea

A CELEBRATION OF PROMISES

*You are invited to rejoice in the promise
of a shared future.
Join us for a tea for the lovely bride-to-be.*

June is a happy month. It sings an announcement of summer pleasures up ahead. The gaiety of spring's charm still dances in the early morning, but by afternoon everyone knows it is indeed a new season. And love is in the air. Many people select this month of contentment as the backdrop for their wedding day.

By June, engaged couples have spent the past few months meeting with ministers, coordinating with caterers, and fantasizing with florists. And now they are ready to be united as husband and wife. Because schedules get so crazy right before a wedding, plan a bridal tea as far in advance as possible so that the bride can look forward to an afternoon of friendly chatter and a bit of pampering in the middle of the hustle and bustle that leads to wedded bliss.

This special tea can include the bridesmaids and a few good friends of the bride. Be sure to include the bride and groom's mothers, grandmothers, and any other relatives she would want invited. With this guest list, some women may not know the others. As a good hostess, you can help everyone get comfortable and connected right away.

Dazzle the bride-to-be and shower her with love.

Recipes

CUCUMBER AND EGG SANDWICHES

5 eggs, hard-boiled, shelled
2 tablespoons whole-grain
    Dijon mustard
¼ cup mayonnaise
1 cucumber, thinly sliced
1 small bunch watercress
12 slices of white bread
12 slices of wheat bread

Chop eggs and blend with mustard and mayonnaise. Spread white bread slices with egg mixture and cucumber slices. Top with wheat bread slices. Trim off crusts and cut each sandwich into four squares. Arrange on plate and garnish with watercress leaves. Can be assembled up to 6 hours ahead and refrigerated. Makes 48 finger sandwiches.

RASPBERRY JAM SANDWICHES

1 jar raspberry jam
1 loaf white bread
salted butter, softened
thinly sliced ham
garnish

Spread thin layer of raspberry jam onto one slice of bread. Spread a thin layer of butter on the other slice of bread. Add 2 slices of ham, close sandwich. Cut out shapes using various patterns of cookie cutters (omit crust). Arrange on tray, garnish around sandwiches with flowers, mint, or sliced orange rind.

COCONUT WEDDING CAKE

1 package (2-layer size) yellow cake mix
1 package (4-serving size) Jell-O brand
    vanilla flavor instant pudding
    and pie filling
1⅓ cups of water
4 eggs
¼ cup of oil
2 cups angel flake coconut
1 cup chopped walnuts or pecans

Blend cake mix, pudding mix, water, eggs, and oil in large mixer bowl. Beat at medium speed of electric mixer 4 minutes. Stir in coconut and walnuts. Pour into 3 greased and floured 9" layer pans. Bake at 350° for 35 minutes. Cool in pans 15 minutes; remove and cool on rack. Fill and top with Coconut-Cream Cheese Frosting (p. 34).

Two souls with but a single thought, two hearts that beat as one.

JOHN KEATS

Sachets for the Bride

A craft project is a clever way to spark conversation and laughter. Have a table set up with all the materials your guests will need to make traditional rice sachets or a more common version with birdseed.

2 pounds white uncooked rice or birdseed
a roll of white wedding netting
3 pairs of scissors
1 roll of white ribbon

Have the netting cut into squares 6" x 6". Place 3 tablespoons of rice in the middle of each square. Fold up the edges of the netting together. Tie with a length of white ribbon 6" long. Place each completed sachet into a beautiful, linen-lined basket. Present the basket to the soon-to-be bride for her wedding.

Susan Rios

COCONUT-CREAM CHEESE FROSTING

4 tablespoons butter or margarine
2 cups angel flake coconut
1 8-ounce package cream cheese
2 teaspoons milk
3½ cups sifted confectioners sugar
½ teaspoon vanilla

Melt 2 tablespoons butter in skillet. Add coconut; stir constantly over low heat until golden brown. Spread coconut on absorbent paper to cool. Cream 2 tablespoons butter with cream cheese. Add milk; beat in sugar gradually. Blend in vanilla; stir in 1¾ cups of coconut. Spread on tops of cake layers. Stack on plate and sprinkle with remaining coconut. High altitude areas: increase water to 1¾ cups and add ¼ cup flour.

RASPBERRY TEA

Prepare your favorite tea.
Raspberry jam

In the bottom of each tea cup, add teaspoon of raspberry jam. Pour hot tea over jam. With spoon stir jam into tea.

Fergie's Cup of Tea

I love America and Americans. So I'm going to put this in the nicest way possible. Not all of you know how to make tea properly. (Of course I don't mean you, dear reader, but you know whom I *do* mean.) This is the English way, the way I do it:

1. First, I make sure that the water is boiling. Not tepid, not merely scalding, but boiling. Just as it begins to boil, I pour a bit of it into my teapot and leave it there a minute to warm up the pot.
2. Then I put the kettle back on, and while I'm waiting for it to boil again, I throw the hot water out of my now-warmed teapot and put in a couple of teaspoons of whatever tea I feel like. I always use loose tea—never bags—it's much tastier.
3. I let the water come to a boil again and pour a little of it over the tea, just enough to wet the tea so it begins to warm and soak a bit. I wait a minute, then I add the rest of the boiling water and let it steep from three to five minutes, depending on how strong I want it.
4. I then pour it into my cup through a tea strainer. I never, ever use a mug or a cup without a saucer. My mum always said that tea tastes much nicer out of a cup and saucer, and goodness, she was right!
5. I take my tea plain—without lemon, milk, or sugar. But if you do use milk, put it in last because it's much more elegant that way. Now do all this, and I guarantee you'll have a proper cup of tea.

SARAH FERGUSON, *The Duchess of York*

A Touch of Inspiration

When our daughter, Jenny, announced her engagement, so many of our friends who had known her from childhood indicated their excitement by wanting to host a tea for her. Sue, a close friend, offered her home for this tea to remember. Sue's creative flair is evident throughout her home. Her many beautiful tea pieces collected over the years are part of her home's decor and are symbols of her hospitable heart.

For this bride and bridesmaid tea, Jenny was able to invite her six bridesmaids, the mothers of the bride and groom, and a few selected friends. In all, about 14 guests participated. We were all seated around large tables with beautiful lace cloths. Roses freshly cut from Sue's garden adorned every table. Each place setting had a cup and saucer personally selected from the hostess's collection.

As conversation began, we shared what Jenny had meant to us. Each woman shared fond memories and episodes about how she had met our lovely daughter. The older women were able to give golden words of encouragement to her—words that lifted her up as she anticipated this new chapter in her life.

Everyone went home with a tiny teaspoon to remember this wonderful occasion. I still have my little silver spoon 20 years later.

I share this personal experience because it made such an impression on me and those in attendance. Sue's attention to every detail created a splendid afternoon of delight. All felt welcome and pampered; it was truly a celebration of Jenny's future and promise of love. You too can create a lasting memory for a special bride. A little tea, a touch of tradition, and a happily-ever-after toast.

Tea, the Cure-all

If you are cold, tea will warm you;
if you are too heated, it will cool you;
if you are depressed, it will cheer you;
if you are exhausted, it will calm you.

WILLIAM GLADSTONE

July

An Independence Day Tea

A
Celebration
of Freedom

Your family is requested to join our
family at our annual
Fourth of July Beach Party.
We guarantee a bang-up affair!

This is our grand national holiday—the glorious Fourth, when Americans manifest their patriotic enthusiasm in various ways.

The earliest celebration in 1776 was a very exciting and cheerful occasion. At last the colonies were independent from England. People yelled and screamed, lit bonfires, and paraded and danced in the streets.

The Fourth of July is still celebrated in much the same fashion: with parades, dancing, and fireworks (some communities are placing certain restrictions due to possible fire dangers). Since the Fourth of July falls in the summertime and children are out of school, parents can take their families on outings in the park, in the country, or to the seashore.

As you and your family celebrate this day, you can elect to be an originator of traditions in your family, or you may elect to join in other people's traditions. Either way, it is a wonderful time of the year.

Menu for an
Independence Day Picnic
Pasta Salad Supreme
Flag Cake
Banana-Walnut Ice Cream
Fresh Lemonade

Recipes

PASTA SALAD SUPREME

1 pound thin spaghetti
1 8-ounce bottle Italian salad dressing
1 jar Salad Supreme seasoning
2 chopped celery stalks
1 chopped green pepper
1 thinly sliced onion
1 pint cherry tomatoes
1 6-ounce can pitted ripe olives

Cook spaghetti according to package directions. Drain and rinse in cold water. Combine spaghetti, dressing, and seasoning. Add celery, green pepper, and onion. Chill 3 to 4 hours (may do 3 to 4 days ahead). Just before serving, add tomatoes and olives. Makes 8 servings.

FLAG CAKE (SERVE WITH PRIDE!)

1 white cake mix
1 cup heavy cream
1 tablespoon sugar
$\frac{1}{2}$ teaspoon vanilla

$\frac{1}{2}$ cup fresh blueberries
2 cups sliced fresh strawberries

Mix and bake cake according to package directions in 9" x 13" baking dish. Place cake on attractive serving dish or platter. Beat cream until soft peaks form. Add sugar and vanilla. Spread whipped cream in an even layer over top of cake. Place 2 lines of blueberries at right angles in top left corner to form a 4-inch square. Fill square with additional lines of blueberries. Leave small amount of white cream showing between the berries. Use overlapping sliced strawberries to form horizontal red stripes from side to side on cake, allowing cream to show for white stripes. Refrigerate until serving time. Makes 12 to 15 servings.

BANANA-WALNUT ICE CREAM

4 cups sour cream
4 cans sweetened condensed milk
8 cups half-and-half (may use half milk)
6 mashed or chopped bananas
1 cup chopped walnuts

Mix all ingredients. Process in ice-cream freezer for 30 minutes. Makes 1 gallon.

FRESH LEMONADE

For each cup of water, use:

3-4 tablespoons sugar
$1\frac{1}{2}$ tablespoons lemon juice

Boil water and sugar 2 minutes. Chill. Add lemon juice.

A Touch of Inspiration

As we gather our family together for this patriotic day, we journey away from the typical tea of china, lace, silver, and linens. Today's tea is transformed into a picnic. We go to the backyard, to the beach, to the lake, to the mountains—wherever we want to gather together. Our group can be small, or it can really get large. Red, white, and blue become our theme colors.

Your banners, napkins, cups, tablecloths, and balloons can all be decked out in the theme colors. You could even request that your guests wear the theme colors. Make sure you have plenty of film because this will be a tea long to remember. You might even consider having a few disposable cameras available for the children. They love to take pictures, and though sometimes we adults are reluctant to trust them with the camera, today is their day to be expert photographers.

Be sure to send your invitations at least four weeks ahead of the date. People make plans early and need time to decide what they are going to do. Ask your family for suggestions about what the menu will be, what games will be played, and who should be on the guest list.

Write the invitation in white ink on a red card outlined with blue-and-gold star stickers. A small American flag may be included.

Create a firecracker invitation by covering an empty tissue roll with red paper. Information is inside and attached to an 8-inch wick of heavy string with a tag that reads "Pull." Hand deliver.

Line the entrance of your home with several American flags to greet guests with a patriotic spirit. Clusters of red, white, and blue balloons with crepe paper streamers can decorate the party area.

Cover the buffet table with a red or white tablecloth. Bind paper napkins with napkin rings made of white construction paper affixed with a large gold star. Red and white paper plates and cups complete the table setting.

After what I owe to God, nothing should
be more dear or more sacred than
the love and respect I owe to my country.

DE THOU

Old-Fashioned Fun

Independence Day is a festive, fun celebration and ideal for games and activities. Ask the grandparents what kinds of games they used to play when they were young. These older and often-forgotten games are a delight. One such old game is called "pick-up sticks" or "Jack straws." Cut any number of sticks of wood ½" x ½" x 14" and paint them three different colors—red, white, and blue. Throw them in a basket or drop them on the ground in a pile. Ask the children to remove one stick at a time without moving the other sticks. Have colorful prizes for the winners.

Other ideas for your family and neighbors include: sack races, egg toss, and three-legged race.

Here are two new traditions your family might enjoy.

Have a family parade. The children will love this! Get pots and pans, tambourines, horns, and toy instruments. Small children can carry a flag or tie colored balloons onto strollers, wagons, and tricycles. Everyone could march around the neighborhood and ask others to join in the fun. End the parade with a hot-dog roast or an ice cream social.

Plant a tree. Decide beforehand what kind of tree you want to plant. Where do you want to plant it—at home, at church, in a city park, or at school? (If you don't plant it at home, be sure to get permission.) Make sure you know who will take care of the tree. This provides a great opportunity to talk to your children about ecology and is a wonderful way to share a sense of history and future with your growing family.

Independence Day Tradition

THE MILITARY MARKS INDEPENDENCE DAY BY FIRING A SALUTE OF 13 GUNS AND READING THE DECLARATION OF INDEPENDENCE. ALL OVER THE COUNTRY, CHURCHES RING BELLS IN MEMORY OF THE LIBERTY BELL THAT PROCLAIMED INDEPENDENCE. THIS MOST-FAMOUS BELL WAS ACTUALLY MADE IN ENGLAND, AND AROUND ITS RIM ARE THESE PROPHETIC WORDS: "PROCLAIM LIBERTY THROUGHOUT THE LAND UNTO ALL THE INHABITANTS THEREOF."

August

A Birthday Tea

A
CELEBRATION
OF YOU

Since your birthday falls in August,
you are cordially
invited to attend a special tea
just for August birthdays.

A birthday deserves special praise and recognition! Don't you just love celebrating the unique and wonderful people who have added joy to your life and to others'? A birthday celebration warrants lots of creative energy, personal touches, and thoughtful planning to focus on that person's special qualities.

Sometimes the most significant traditions are born out of hard times. After my father's death, my mother was always busy with serving customers, doing alterations, and keeping books to support us. Birthday parties were not a priority. So when I was 12, I gave myself my first birthday party. I gave out invitations, cleaned the house, baked a cake, cut flowers, and put up streamers. My friends came and brought presents. I was so embarrassed that I hid in the closet and wouldn't come out. The adult in me could plan the party and organize the attention, but when it came, I was overwhelmed. It was then that I decided to make birthdays special for my children someday. And believe me...birthdays are always a great cause for celebration in our home.

Birthdays provide a wonderful excuse to have a party any month of the year. Prepare a grand celebration this month for friends, family, and neighbors who are ready to blow out the candles and rejoice in the gift of life.

Recipes

SUGAR SCONES

2 cups flour
1 teaspoon baking powder
$^1/_4$ cup butter
5 teaspoons sugar
$^2/_3$ cup milk
1 teaspoon vanilla

Preheat oven to 425°. Dust a baking sheet with flour. Sift flour and baking powder into a mixing bowl and then stir to mix. Add butter; then stir in sugar. Make a well in the center of the dry mixture. Add milk and vanilla, mixing it in until dough is soft but not sticky. Turn out dough onto a floured surface and knead lightly. Pat dough out to one inch thick. Using round cookie cutter, cut out 12 scones. Arrange on floured baking sheet and dust the tops of the scones with flour. Bake 12 minutes or until lightly browned. Serves 12.
Serve with Devonshire Mock Cream.

DEVONSHIRE MOCK CREAM

1 cup heavy cream (not pasteurized)
1 8-ounce softened cream cheese
2 tablespoons powdered sugar

Beat ingredients together in a bowl. It mixes together quickly. Serves 12.

HONEY-SMOKED TURKEY SANDWICHES

$^1/_2$ cup unsalted butter, softened
2 teaspoons orange juice concentrate
1 teaspoon ginger root, grated
1 loaf white bread
$^1/_2$ pound honey-smoked turkey, thinly sliced

Add ginger to juice. In a bowl, whisk together butter and juice. Spread a thin layer of orange butter on a slice of bread and place a slice of smoked turkey on top. Cut bread into fourths. You can cut using cookie cutter for unique design. Serves 10.

Birthday Tradition

The practice of marking an individual's exact date of birth came into existence only with the recording of time by a fixed calendar. Originally, birthdays were not celebrated by commoners. It has only been in recent times that general populations have celebrated individual birthdays.

EMILIE'S TRIPLE-CHOCOLATE FUDGE CAKE

This is so easy and so good, a hit with every bite!
You may want to have it at every tea party!

1 small package chocolate pudding mix
    (not instant)
1 box chocolate cake mix (dry mix)
1/2 cup semisweet chocolate pieces
1/2 cup chopped nuts
whipped cream

Cook pudding as directed on package, and blend dry cake mix into hot pudding. (Mixture will be thick.) Pour into prepared pan (13" x 9½" x 2") and sprinkle with chocolate pieces and nuts. Bake 30 to 35 minutes at 350°. Cool 5 minutes, cut into 2-inch squares, and arrange on cake plate or doily-lined tray. Serve plain or topped with a dollop of whipped cream.

A Touch of Inspiration

Parties with themes can be a lot of fun and will flow smoothly because you have a definite plan. When celebrating birthdays for all ages, add whimsical decorations to every corner of your home: a bouquet of balloons, bowls of colorfully wrapped candies, streamers in metallic shades, banners, larger-than-life homemade birthday cards for everyone at the party to sign, and plenty of noisemakers, hats, and food!

At the August party the birthday guests will likely vary in age. Include games and icebreakers that suit each age group represented. The fun will cross all generations! Create crowns out of poster board and foil for the birthday boys, girls, men, and women to wear. Roll out a red carpet, or a red-paper carpet, leading to a head table where the guests of honor can sit in the royal limelight. Decorate each of their chairs with stickers, balloons, even fabric for a rich, festive feel. Have lots of costume jewelry handy to adorn the women and girls. Match the men's and boys' crowns with scepters made out of paper towel rolls and foil. Let your house glitter with twinkle lights and shiny confetti.

Birthdays deserve the royal treatment. Bestow upon your aging guests the treasures of friendship and good memories. Every person and every season of a person's life deserves to be celebrated!

Birthday Party Icebreakers

- Have the guests share their first name and a word that describes themselves using the first letter of their name (for example: "My name is Kari and I am kind.").
- Have guests introduce themselves by telling their favorite color, favorite TV program, favorite food, when they were born, etc.
- Go around the room and have each person share two lies and one truth about themselves. Let others guess which one of the three is the truth.

You created every part of me; you put me together in my mother's womb. I praise you because you are to be feared; all you do is strange and wonderful. I know it with all my heart. When my bones were being formed, carefully put together in my mother's womb, when I was growing there in secret, you knew that I was there—you saw me before I was born. The days allotted to me had all been recorded in your book, before any of them ever began.

PSALM 139:13-16 (TEV)

September

A Chocolate Lover's Tea

A Celebration of Sweet Pleasures

Come to a delightful Chocolate Tea.
Your palate will be thrilled you brought it.

This is the tea that all my friends want to be invited to. In a day and age where slimness is in, we ladies want to indulge in the greatest forbidden dessert—chocolate.

We are not surprised that chocolate is one of our favorite ways to say "I love you" to ourselves and to others. This treat contains phenylethylamine, the same chemical that our brain releases when we fall in love. While we cannot quite label chocolate a health food, in moderation it does have some components that can be good for us. I would say the smile factor alone is a health benefit, wouldn't you?

When chocolate becomes the actual theme for a gathering, your guests will simply adore you. Any leftovers will gladly be taken home. There will be no crumbs left on the plates. And everyone will want to know the recipe of their evening's favorite treat.

Know also that wisdom is sweet to your soul; if you find it, there is a future hope for you.

PROVERBS 24:14

45

Emily Post Says

The tea pouring is usually done by close friends of the hostess. These ladies are asked beforehand if they will "do the honors," and unless they have a very valid reason, they should accept. Sometimes, after an hour, the first two are relieved by two other friends of the hostess.

It does not matter that a guest going into the dining room does not know the deputy hostesses who are pouring. Each person walks right up to the table and says, "May I have a cup of tea?"

The one pouring should smile and answer, "Certainly! How do you like it? Strong or weak? Would you like cream or lemon?"

If the visitor says, "Weak," boiling water is added, and according to the guest's wishes, sugar, cream, or lemon.

ELIZABETH I. POST   *The New Emily Post Etiquette*

Recipes

CHOCOLATE CAKE TORTA

German chocolate cake mix (and
required ingredients for preparation)
1½ cups vanilla wafer crumbs
1½ cups walnuts or pecans chopped
1½ cups brown sugar
1 cup melted butter
2 cups wipped cream

Preheat oven at 350°. Prepare the German chocolate cake mix and set aside. Mix the remaining wafer ingredients together. Divide into three 8" cake pans that are greased and floured. Line them with waxed paper over the grease and flour. Pour in the vanilla wafer mixture first, then the cake mix. Bake for 30-35 minutes. Cool 19 minutes, then turn out cakes. Layer cake with whipped cream in between layers. Refrigerate for 1 hour. Serves 12.

Teatime is by its very nature a combination of small luxuries arranged in a sociable setting.
EMILIE BARNES

GIANT CHOCOLATE CHIP COOKIES

2½ cups all-purpose flour
1 teaspoon baking soda
1 teaspoon salt
½ cup (1 stick) unsalted butter,
room temperature
½ cup solid vegetable shortening
¾ cup sugar
¾ cup (packed) golden brown sugar
1 tablespoon sour cream
1½ teaspoons vanilla extract
2 large eggs
1 pound (2⅔ cups) semi-sweet
chocolate chips
½ cup chopped walnuts (optional)

Preheat oven to 350°. Sift flour, baking soda, and salt into medium bowl. Using electric mixer, beat butter and vegetable shortening in large bowl until fluffy. Add sugar, brown sugar, sour cream, and vanilla. Beat to blend well. Beat in eggs one at a time; then add flour mixture. Stir in chocolate chips and walnuts. Drop batter by generous ¼ cupfuls onto 2 large ungreased baking sheets (5 mounds per sheet, spaced 3 inches apart). Using moistened fingertips flatten each mound to 2½" round. Bake cookies until golden brown (about 14 minutes). Cool on sheets for 5 minutes. Transfer cookies to racks and cool completely. Repeat with remaining batter using cooled baking sheets. Serves 20.

ROCKY ROAD CLUSTERS

2 cups (12 ounce package) Nestlé
Toll House Semi-Sweet
Chocolate Morsels
1¼ cups (14-ounce can) Carnation
Sweetened Condensed Milk
2½ cups miniature marshmallows
1 cup coarsely chopped nuts
1 teaspoon vanilla extract

Combine morsels and sweetened condensed milk in large microwave-safe bowl. Microwave on high (100%) power for 1 minute; stir until smooth. If necessary, microwave for 20-30 seconds longer to complete melting. Stir in marshmallows, nuts, and vanilla. Drop by heaping tablespoons into mounds on waxed paper. Chill until firm. Serves 24.

MINT CHOCOLATE SANDWICH COOKIES

¼ cup plus 1½ teaspoons vegetable
shortening, divided
½ cup sugar
¼ cup unsweetened cocoa
3 tablespoons milk
1 teaspoon vanilla extract
1 teaspoon mint extract, divided
¼ teaspoon baking soda
⅔ cup all-purpose flour
6 ounces white chocolate squares

Heat oven to 375°. Beat together ¼ cup shortening, sugar, cocoa, milk, vanilla, and half of the mint extract in a large mixer bowl on medium speed until combined. Add baking soda and as much of the flour as you can. Stir in the remaining flour by hand until combined. Shape the dough into a ball. Divide dough in half. On a lightly floured surface, roll each half 1/16 inch thick. Cut out with 2-inch heart-shaped cookie cutters. Place on ungreased cookie sheets and bake 4 to 5 minutes or until edges are firm. Cool on cookie sheets for 1 minute. Transfer to wire rack and cool completely. Melt white chocolate and 1½ teaspoons of shortening in the top of a double boiler over low heat, stirring often. Remove from heat. Stir in remaining mint extract and cool slightly. Transfer mixture to a small heavy duty plastic storage bag. Snip a ¼-inch corner from the bag. Working quickly, pipe about 1 teaspoon of white chocolate mixture on top of half of the cookies. Top each iced cookie with a second cookie. Decoratively pipe mixture on top if desired. Makes 15 cookies.

APPLE-MINT TEA

2 cups apple juice
1 quart water
1 cup chopped fresh mint leaves

Mix the ingredients together and bring to a boil. Add 6 teaspoons loose tea or 6 to 8 tea bags of your basic tea choice. Steep 5 minutes. Ready to serve.

A Touch of Inspiration

Quite often it is the little luxuries in life that mean the most and provide the greatest comfort and pleasure. Tea at any hour of the day is a welcomed respite to the mind, body, and soul. Regardless of the time of day, the teapot is always the star of the table setting. Select your coziest of teacups to highlight the decor of the teapot. Your silver, linens, and flowers will accentuate the teapot. Mix and match without the worry of all items being the same.

A cheery bunch of flower-shaped, chocolate temptations on stems can be arranged as your centerpiece. These are also easy to make. Candy molds are available in the shape of roses, tulips, and many other blooms. Generously display candy kisses on the table and on every surface in your living room. After all, you don't want people to have to go far for their favorite sweet! If children will be present, consider planning a September Easter egg hunt. Fill plastic eggs with small chocolate delights and hide them around the room or even in the yard. This will be a fun, surprise activity for everyone at any point during the tea.

Before the guests arrive, have hot cocoa already made and melting chocolate on the stove. As your friends enter and smell the aroma of heaven, happiness will abound. Have classical music playing softly in the background to create a peaceful, relaxing, and conversation-friendly atmosphere. You are stirring up memories that your guests will savor for years to come.

Chocolate Tips

• Chocolate shavings add a beautiful and delicious touch to your dessert. To shave chocolate, pull a vegetable peeler across the surface of a square of semi-sweet chocolate.

• Chocolate should be melted gently to prevent scorching. Using the microwave is a quick and easy way to melt chocolate. Place chocolate in a small microwavable container and microwave at high about 60 seconds per ounce of chocolate. The chocolate will retain its shape even when almost melted, so stir it several times during the process.

• Unsweetened chocolate is often called bitter chocolate or baking chocolate. It is the purest form of chocolate with no added flavors or sugar. It is used for baking because of the bitter taste. It is available in packages of individually wrapped 1-ounce squares.

October

An Autumn Tea

A Celebration of the Harvest

May you join me for a festive fall tea.
Apples are on the trees and
pumpkins are on the vine.
Come and share the bounty.

What a wonderful month October is! The heat and humidity of summer have gone away. September has brought us back to a normal lifestyle, the children have returned to school, and life for a short time has begun to mellow. I sense the feel of autumn in the air. The trees start their gorgeous parade of reds, yellows, and oranges. Our thoughts go to crackling fires in the fireplace, shorter days, and more time for cozying up on the couch to immerse yourself in a good book. Even those who do not typically sit with a cup of tea will find themselves longing to sit with friends while sipping this soothing balm for the soul.

Tea is a perfect complement in the fall and winter months. Plan to share the sights and smells of the harvest. Invite a small gathering of friends in from the cold to bask in the warmth of autumn's soothing embrace.

Recipes

APPLE CIDER TEA

2½ teaspoons black tea leaves
2½ cups water
¼ cup sugar
juice of two oranges (about 1 cup)
5 cups apple cider
8 thin lemon slices

Following the traditional method, make tea from tea leaves and boiling water; allow to brew for 5 minutes. Place sugar in a large bowl or pitcher. Strain hot tea into bowl and stir until sugar is dissolved. Stir in orange juice. Just before serving, add apple cider and reheat. Pour into cups and offer a slice of lemon for each guest. Serves 10.

APPLE BREAD PUDDING

5 large slices country-style rustic bread, stale preferred
¾ cup milk
5 apples, such as Golden Delicious or Gala
¼ cup sugar
grated peel of 1 lemon
⅓ cup chopped walnuts (toasted 8 to 10 minutes in a 350° oven)

1 egg, room temperature
1 teaspoon vanilla extract
1 tablespoon butter

Preheat oven to 350°. Grease a 9½" baking dish, such as a soufflé dish, with butter. Break up bread into 1-inch chunks and put into a large bowl. Pour milk over bread and set aside to soften. Peel and core apples and cut them into thin slices. Add them to bread-milk mixture. Add sugar, lemon peel, and walnuts. Beat egg and vanilla. Stir into bread mixture. Spread mixture into prepared dish. Cut butter into tiny pieces and scatter over top of apple mixture. Bake 60 to 75 minutes, until apple slices are tender and the top is lightly crunchy and golden. Serve warm. Serves 12.

CREAM CHEESE SANDWICHES

½ loaf thinly sliced white bread
½ loaf thinly sliced whole-wheat bread
½ cup butter room temperature
1 pound cream cheese, softened

Trim crusts from bread. Lightly spread butter and cream cheese on 1 side of each slice. Stack 4 slices, alternating white and whole-wheat bread. Stack first 3 slices filled-side up, then set top slice in place filled-side down. Repeat with remaining bread slices. Wrap in foil and refrigerate at least 1 hour. To serve, cut stacks in strips about ½ inch wide, slicing through all 4 layers. Arrange on plate with striped side up. Makes 30 fingers.

CARAMELIZED WALNUT TART

refrigerated pie crust (half of 15-ounce
   package)
$\frac{1}{2}$ cup whipping cream
$\frac{1}{2}$ cup golden brown sugar
$\frac{1}{4}$ cup dark corn syrup
1 teaspoon vanilla extract
$\frac{1}{2}$ teaspoon ground cinnamon
$1\frac{1}{4}$ cups coarsely chopped roasted
   walnuts

Preheat oven to 400°. Transfer crust to 9"
tart pan with removable bottom, folding in
overhang to form double-thick sides. Freeze
crust while preparing filling. Whisk cream,
sugar, corn syrup, vanilla, and cinnamon in
large heavy saucepan. Stir in walnuts.
Simmer over medium heat until mixture is
bubbling and darkens slightly, stirring until
sugar dissolves, about 3 minutes. Spread
filling evenly in crust. Bake tart until filling
is deep golden brown and crust is golden,
about 25 minutes. Cool completely in pan on
rack. Remove tart from pan and serve. Makes
6 servings.

Come, ye thankful people, come,
Raise the song of harvest home;
All is safely gathered in,
Ere the winter storms begin.
HENRY ALFORD

A Classic Touch

Let music swirl about your guests like the falling leaves outside. Music is an invitation to traditions of gracious splendor.

Ludwig van Beethoven, *The Late Quartets,* the Budapest Quartet, Columbia/Odyssey Y4 34644 (not yet transferred to CD).

Wolfgang Amadeus Mozart, *String Quartets 1-16,* the Hungarian Quartet, EMI CZST 67236-2.

Franz Joseph Haydn, *The Haydn Quartets,* the Chilingirian Quartet, CRD 3362-3364.

Franz Joseph Haydn, *The Haydn Quartets,* the Salomon Quartet, Hyperion CDS 440013.

A Touch of Inspiration

As your guests arrive, the smell of cinnamon sticks and water simmering on the stove effectively ushers them into your home. For a dash of colorful charm, decorate with those wonderful elements that one associates with fall: autumn leaves, appropriate flowers, apples, pumpkins, and cones and burrs fallen from the trees.

Create different levels on your main table for an interesting presentation. You might continue this theme and design for other areas in your home. Line up a few small pots of flowers on a windowsill and be sure to place arrangements in other rooms the guests will visit.

If you have a fireplace, be sure to stack up the wood and have the flames aglow. Soft background music sets a very soothing atmosphere. Candles in scents of cinnamon, spice, vanilla, and pine add a touch of rustic bliss to your perfectly inviting home.

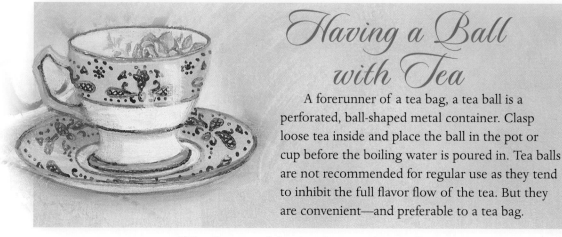

Having a Ball with Tea

A forerunner of a tea bag, a tea ball is a perforated, ball-shaped metal container. Clasp loose tea inside and place the ball in the pot or cup before the boiling water is poured in. Tea balls are not recommended for regular use as they tend to inhibit the full flavor flow of the tea. But they are convenient—and preferable to a tea bag.

"The Spirits of the Air live on the smells

Of fruit, and Joy, with pinions light, roves round

The gardens, or sits singing in the trees."

Thus sang the jolly Autumn as he sat;

Then rose, girded himself, and o'er the bleak

Hills fled from our sight; but left his golden load.

WILLIAM BLAKE

November

A Thanksgiving Tea

A CELEBRATION OF BLESSINGS

*A seasonal tea has been planned
just for you.
Bring with you a special
Thanksgiving memory to share.*

Ah, November. In many parts of our country, the first snowfall has painted strokes of white across once-green lawns. The days are cold and the remembrances of a warm day are long forgotten. Now is the time to place a log in the fireplace, have a few friends over, sit down for a couple of hours, and get caught up with the latest. Just the idea of Thanksgiving casts the days in a warm glow. So set your tea date so that it won't interfere with family activities for the month, and prepare for a seasonal celebration that is sure to become a tradition.

For the last 100 years in America, we have begun to develop some meaningful traditions to make this one of the most memorable holidays: family gatherings, celebration of our national heritage, decorative settings, and favorite recipes passed through generations. When a feast of thanksgiving is prepared, even the simplest meal or tea feeds more than physical appetites. It feeds the soul.

Gratitude is infectious. Before you get caught up in the last details of this tea, write down five of your greatest blessings. Your heart will be filled as you create a place of welcome, care, and appreciation for your chosen guests. The atmosphere you nurture will radiate the spirit of this beautiful season and will cultivate a sense of tradition for those seated at your table.

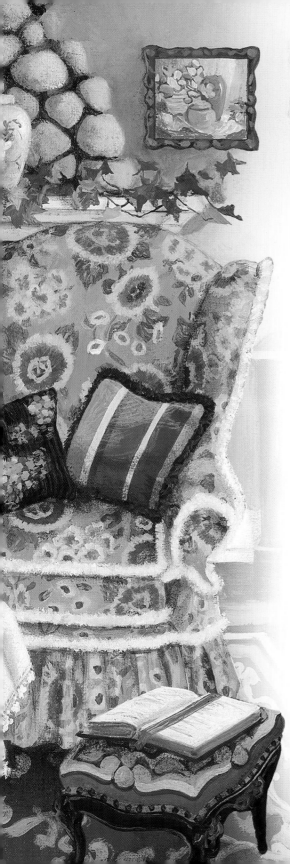

Recipes

ORANGE MUFFINS

$\frac{1}{3}$ cup dried cranberries, chopped

$\frac{1}{3}$ cup plus 2 tablespoons sugar

3 tablespoons boiling water

$1\frac{3}{4}$ cups all-purpose flour

$\frac{1}{2}$ cup yellow cornmeal

$2\frac{1}{2}$ teaspoons baking powder

$\frac{1}{2}$ teaspoon baking soda

$\frac{1}{2}$ teaspoon salt

2 eggs

1 cup milk

$\frac{1}{3}$ cup unsalted butter, melted

1 tablespoon grated orange peel

Preheat oven to 400°. In a small bowl, stir together cranberries and 2 tablespoons sugar. Stir in boiling water; set aside for 15 minutes to soften cranberries. In a large bowl, mix flour, cornmeal, $\frac{1}{3}$ cup sugar, baking powder, baking soda, and salt. In another bowl, using a whisk, beat eggs lightly. Add milk and melted butter; beat until smooth. Stir in cranberries, their liquid, and grated orange peel. Stir liquid mixture into flour mixture. Divide batter evenly among buttered muffin cups, filling each ¾ full. Bake at 400° until risen and the tops are golden (15 to 20 minutes). Remove from the oven and let cool in pan for 2 to 3 minutes. Serve warm. Makes 12 muffins.

57

PUMPKIN WAFFLES

½ cup canned pumpkin
3 eggs, well beaten
1½ cups milk
2 tablespoons melted butter
1 cup all-purpose flour, sifted
2 teaspoons baking powder
½ teaspoon salt
2 tablespoons sugar
⅛ teaspoon nutmeg

Stir together pumpkin, eggs, milk, and butter. In a separate bowl, combine flour, baking powder, salt, sugar, and nutmeg. Add dry ingredients to pumpkin mixture. Stir until thoroughly combined. Cook according to the directions for your waffle maker. Serve immediately with berry or maple syrup, fresh berries, or ginger whipped cream. Serves 4.

TURKEY-FILLED SANDWICHES

1 pound turkey breast
1 large dill pickle
6 hard-boiled eggs
2 teaspoons mustard
3 tablespoons mayonnaise
salt and pepper to taste
white or whole-wheat bread

Combine turkey, pickle, eggs, and mustard in food processor. Moisten with mayonnaise. Spread on white or whole-wheat bread. Trim crusts off bread. Cut into squares. Ready to serve (keep refrigerated until ready to serve). Makes 20 squares.

I will praise God's name in song and glorify him with thanksgiving.
PSALM 69:30

HOT BUTTERED CRANBERRY CIDER

⅓ cup butter, softened
⅓ cup mild honey
½ teaspoon ginger
½ teaspoon cinnamon
1 48-ounce bottle cranberry juice
   cocktail
1 quart cider
cinnamon sticks (optional)

Blend softened butter, honey, and spices. This may be done ahead of time. When ready to serve, combine cranberry cocktail and cider. Bring to a boil or heat in a party percolator. Have butter mixture beside the pot. To serve, put a small spoonful of honey-butter in each mug or heat-proof punch cup. Fill with hot cranberry cider. Stir with a cinnamon stick. Serves 10.

Let us observe this day with reverence and with prayer that will rekindle in us the will and show us the way not only to preserve our blessings, but also to extend them to the four corners of the earth.

JOHN F. KENNEDY,
Thanksgiving Proclamation, 1961

A Touch of Inspiration

Nature's November rainbow makes an excellent color scheme for a Thanksgiving tea. Orange, brown, auburn, and golden yellows found among twigs, leaves, fruit, and small pumpkins can become your centerpiece and seasonal palette throughout the house. Bring out a fall tablecloth as a perfect accent. Duplicate the same feel with other tables you may have around the room. Orange candles will illuminate every detail. Check with your florist or market for appropriate potted flowers. This is one of my favorite teas. It really brings out the warmth of the season.

For a very personal and meaningful touch, take a 3" x 5" card, fold it in half, and stand it on the table. On the front write the name of the person who will sit at that place, and inside write a Thanksgiving Scripture. When everyone is seated, each person then reads her verse—that can be the table blessing. Another variation for this is to place a blank 3" x 5" card and a pen at each setting. Then have everyone write something for which they are thankful. These can be read before, during, or after the tea.

Look around the table and take in the bounty of great friends you have been blessed with. Share with them what each person means in your life. This will inspire the most significant tradition of all—counting your blessings.

The Thanksgiving Tradition

The Pilgrims, who in 1621 observed our first Thanksgiving holiday in Plymouth, Massachusetts, were thankful for their harvest in the New World. They had suffered a perilous journey on the Mayflower, a dreadfully cold winter, and a large number of deaths. By most standards, the first harvest was very mediocre. Many of the first crops were failures. This first Thanksgiving lasted for three days and was celebrated with enthusiasm. The menu was extensive and the food abundant. The Native Americans had added five deer to the store of meat. The Pilgrims had venison, duck, goose, seafood, eels, white bread, cornbread, leeks, watercress, and a variety of greens. Wild plums and dried berries were served for dessert. Although turkeys were plentiful, we have no record that they were eaten on this first Thanksgiving holiday.

December

A Christmas Tea

A CELEBRATION OF TRADITIONS

*Please join us for an
old-fashioned holiday party.*

Once a year the Christmas season influences both the sacred and secular segments of life. Christmas is everywhere: on the sides of buses, in malls, on banners, in music, and on the television. For approximately 45 days each year, the world is surrounded by holy images and belief in a love bigger than ourselves.

This unveiling of God's gift of His Son to all of humanity becomes the inspiration for all giving. Light, life, and love echo from deep within, and the world pauses to listen. Traditions resonate with grace, hope, and compassion. Kindness is extended toward one's fellowman, and the impulse to give from the heart and to give sincerely becomes a source of immense joy.

Celebrating the birth of a Savior is the tradition of this holiday. Discover how to share a message of hope and peace with those around you. Let this be a time of traditions steeped in love. This tea is a great place to begin.

Recipes

CHRISTMAS SPICED TEA

Makes 1½ quarts
  1 cup instant tea (dry)
    (can use decaffeinated)
  2 cups dry lemonade mix (orange flavor)
  3 cups sugar (may use 1½ cups sugar
    substitute and 1½ cups sugar)
  ½ cup red hots (candy)
  1 teaspoon cinnamon
  ½ teaspoon powdered cloves
  ½ package dry lemonade mix (8 ounces)

To 1 cup of hot water, add 1 heaping
tablespoon of mix. Serves 30.

TASTY CINNAMON NUTS

  3 cups almond, walnut, peanut,
    or pecan meats
  1 cup sugar
  ½ cup water
  1 teaspoon cinnamon

In a 12" skillet on medium heat, mix all
ingredients together. Cook, stirring continu-
ally, until syrup caramelizes (about 12 to 15
minutes). Bottom of the pan will appear dry.
Scrape pan with the wooden spoon you are
using to stir with until all liquid is gone.
Then spread the coated nuts onto a tin foil-
lined large cookie sheet to cool for a few
minutes. Store in an airtight container.
Wonderful gift for Christmas treats.

The Art of Buttering Crumpets

All crumpets should be toasted on both sides, the smooth side first, the holey side
last, as this produces a suitable concavity for the butter....Never cut a muffin, snip round
the curved side and pull top and bottom apart and insert the butter in thin slices. Do not
attempt to spread it.

DOROTHY HARTLEY *Food in England*

CHRISTMAS CRUMPETS

2 teaspoons yeast
$\frac{1}{2}$ teaspoon salt
1 teaspoon sugar
1 cup flour
$\frac{1}{4}$ cup warm water
$\frac{1}{3}$ cup milk
4 tablespoons butter melted, divided
1 egg, lightly beaten

Mix yeast with sugar; add warm water and let stand approximately 5 minutes. The mixture will be frothy. Stir in 1 tablespoon butter, egg, and milk. Add salt and flour and mix until well blended. Cover bowl with damp dishtowel and let rise in warm place until batter is about twice in size. Grease four 3" flan rings and a heavy frying pan with remaining 3 tablespoons butter. Place flan rings in pan and heat over low to medium heat. Pour about 2 tablespoons of the batter into each ring and cook until holes appear—about 6 minutes. Remove rings, flip crumpets to the other side, and cook another 2 minutes or until bottoms are lightly browned. Repeat with remaining batter. Makes 12.

LEMON CURD

zest of 2 large lemons, finely grated
juice of 2 large lemons
   (strain and remove pulp)
$1\frac{1}{3}$ cups sugar
3 large eggs, slightly beaten
$\frac{1}{3}$ cup butter

Combine zest of lemon, juice, sugar, and eggs in the top of a double boiler. Stir together until well blended. Place pan over simmering water to heat, stirring constantly until thickened—approximately 5 minutes. Do not allow mixture to boil. Remove the top of the double boiler from the hot water and stir in butter until well blended. Store in a container with lid to keep film from forming. Chill until ready to serve. Makes $1\frac{1}{2}$ cups.

A child is born to us!
A son is given to us!
And he will be our ruler.
He will be called, "Wonderful Counselor,"
"Mighty God," "Eternal Father,"
"Prince of Peace."

ISAIAH 9:6 (TEV)

For SANTA

A Touch of Inspiration

Schedule your tea so it falls after you have your holiday decorations up inside and out. Of all my teas I love the setting for December. Somehow it awakens my memories from childhood—the sights, the smells, the music, the family gatherings. Because I came from a Jewish family, we celebrated the eight days of Hanukkah. The warmth and coziness of these traditions arouse a childlike peace and joy in me.

This experience can be an easy one to put off as your To-Do list grows with each passing day. Oh my, the holiday gets so busy! However, experiencing a tea that remembers "The Reason for the Season" models hope to our family and friends.

As friends enter your home, they readily see that you have prepared a place for them. They know you cared enough to invite them. They will witness the message of Christmas in every room and in every word spoken. They can see it, hear it, smell it, and even taste and touch it. You tantalize all their senses because you care for them—your honored guests.

Since this is a celebration of traditions, we want our guests to leave the tea with a few good ideas that they might consider for their own homes. Invite your friends to share traditions they had as children and those traditions they have started with their own families.

The Christmas Tradition

People in a hundred languages sing the joys of Christmas and share their respective country's traditions. Austria gave us "Silent Night"; England contributed the mistletoe ball and wassail; Germany, the Christmas tree; Scandinavia, the Yule candle and Yule log; Mexico, the poinsettia plant. These traditions continue to be celebrated with fresh and innovative ideas.